More Rocks

Straight forward
observations and
various things that
come to his mind.

~~demonstrative~~
denotative (denotation)
goes by the dictionary

MORE ROCKS

Stephen Ratcliffe

Cuneiform Press 2020

Distributed by:
Small Press Distribution
1341 Seventh Street
Berkeley, CA 94710-1409
Tel. (800) 869-7553
www.spdbooks.org

Published by:
Cuneiform Press
www.cuneiformpress.com

For Robert Grenier

cloud, suddenly
there is one and

after that two,
how mitosis

in cells goes on,
how at times one

notices how
another per-

son appears, that
a spark can light

the sky that is
now empty, blue

dome, as above
that mountain that

memory is
thinking of, this

form of being
say, that water

might be falling
behind you, that

sound, an unseen
action off stage

so to speak, as
if one hears it

only, doesn't
visually

see what's going
on elsewhere, one

called Hamlet, one
the person he

is to marry
for instance, or

so his mother
says, the one he

loves but also
gives away, so

to speak, both to
his surrogate

father, the one
who has married

his mother, and
to another

woman, her name
Ophelia

though no one knows
why, perhaps O

phallus or love
of the O, one

is thinking, one
walking toward

the stream warmed by
the sun, as I

sit here, as if
meditation

could be this, back
feels flexible

I see, stretching
first to the side

or should I say
leaning left, lean

sounds good, so
does leaning right

although the sound
is different,

counting differ-
ent syllables

that way, which I
mean to from time

to time, as if
counting something

were anything
special, which it

is but also
isn't, counting

being a part
of everything,

whatever it
is called, perhaps

life force, the spark
I like to say

sometimes, how it
happens when you

least expect it,
or maybe you

know it, that is
if you happen

to be someone
who is perceptive,

feeling, its form
something one can

invent or not,
so much depends

on who one is,
where one comes from

and so on, such
questions being

what someone writes
down, cloud divides

into two wholes,
each one of them

going forward,
a wing behind

the mountain, or
is it that ridge

between something
or something else,

an unnamed peak
I think, but as

for me, helas
I may no more

as Wyatt wrote,
the weathered ship

hath wearied me
so sore, flower

beside the trail
for which I stop,

notice what is
going on, on

stage so to speak,
or rather in

front of me or
off to one side,

three dimension-
ality a

thing that can be
translated, here

for example,
written on this

piece of paper,
that you and I

climb up Piute
Pass, which is like

life itself I
say, paradigm

as someone else
said, not that it's

not my word, as
if sound can be

separated,
an equation

by which someone
divided her-

self from someone
else, one who was

her companion
to say it, so

that one is in-
side someone else

like the bear tear-
ing open his

chest, which is how
his mate gets in

in Inouet
mythology,

Mike said, walking
along the beach

once upon a
time, pelicans

in a feeding
frenzy, as it

is called, this place
having been chosen

as a kind of
home, that a man

could live in say
tonight, the wind

blowing, a few
clouds north of us

above Mt Humphreys,
mosquito at

my ear, airplane
as it fades east

or is that north
of here, hearing

it or not, as
if it matters

to say something,
that another

person might hear
or read it, that

person being
an eye, reader

as opposed to
one who listens,

an ear, that is
the sound of wind

at my ear, for
instance how it

can be taken
to mean itself,

you understand
what I'm saying,

what I mean so
to speak, as we

who love to be
astonished, as

Lyn put it so
suddenly, one

of those things you
think here, meaning

in blue sky, how
light the sun is

at eleven
thousand feet, how

suddenly cold-
er once it's gone

down, like a face
breaking into

a look of sad-
ness for instance

to call it that,
not knowing why

you want to do
or say it, not

imagine that
a story ends,

two people who
fell in love, past

tense, having been
for some time now

essentially
independent,

otherwise con-
tinuous as

the person who
I think is you,

walking into
trees, how the sun

casts its shadow
forward, toward

the way you are
going, how that

stripe on the rock
means direction,

how it is eye
sees itself, I

in relation
to you, as if

mirrored, water
falling over

those rocks, someone
who thinks to say

there is a lake,
beside it tufts

of grass, a few
wild strawberry

beds, let me take
you to the stream

where you can sit,
contemplate it

as if it were
the word "granite,"

dislocated,
like a person

thinking without
commas, one whom

sound is meaning
to think, that I

"itself," more sun
cream on shoulders

as Peter pulls
in a fish, six

inches I'd say,
holds his fingers

up to show me
its dimension,

smiling, the sound
of water that

which pours, as if
a description

of it could e-
qual anything

itself, music
a few numbers

for example,
how lost an ant

gets on granite,
fly on left leg

isn't noticed
that is (passive

voice) now moving
into the future

tense, syllable
that is to say

grammar, the son
who is listening

to his father
who is a ghost,

Hamlet the son
named his father,

murdered as he
lay sleeping, as

was his custom
of the after-

noon, sound asleep
in his orchard

when his brother
came, Claudius

continued at
the next rest, as

music is, that
being that is

a mirror some-
body will see

you in, the last
word on the page

ultra violet
Viola, which

is pronounced Vi-
ola accent

not on the o
but i, vowel

sound, Viola
so the meter

tells us, wooden
bridge across dry

rock canyon, wind
warm from the west

from time to time
all day, as it

has been since when-
ever I climbed

out of my tent
it had started,

beginning down
a canyon, bend

left, where it gets
steeper as it

follows the path
water follows,

descending that
is, gravity

for example,
poetry is

mathematics
also, music

as they say, an
ant on the path

where I will step,
that tree growing

out of the rock,
I like this one

you say, I say
me too before

moving ahead
to the next stop,

an hour walking,
ten minute rest

makes rhythm, a
punctuation

mark so to speak,
you know what I

mean even if
it isn't yours,

these words I mean,
nobody owns

them, no one can
say this word is

mine, and then went
down to the ship

as Pound said, set
keel to breakers

comma, line break
across which eyes

fall, rocks almost
under my foot

that is, how it
is to find camp

after all day
on the trail, one

who sits writing
this, an old log

now a kitchen,
light on the face

of granite knob
facing west, how

sun reflected
off it looks, glows

almost, if that
isn't too much

to say, old trunk
of tree a bit

like me, something
about the way

it happens to
appear, to me

that is, now that
I'm lying down

looking up at
it, how many

needles one way
to know its name,

identity
say, a matter

of genus and
species, as one

returns having
hooked four, landed

two, how the light
once the sun sets

diminishes,
as notes descend

three at a time
to the root, so

called, or tonic
depending on

whom you talk to,
interruption

meaning that time
is passing, this

point different
from that one, three

syllables in
that word, counting

the point where sound
begins, moonlight

being cast be-
hind you spaces

impossible
without it, small

handwriting now
I'm not walking,

more legible
apparently,

or so the eye
thinks, assuming

contradiction
in terms, the bridge

across the south
fork missing, where

it was anchors
fixed in rock, what

else to call them,
the river where

I wash my feet
and calves, and why

not, given that
is possible

gradually,
how the first star

suddenly is
there, another

the next time eye
looks up, meaning

I see it next,
almost too dark

to see, moonlight
filtered behind

thin haze of cloud
moving in, in

that sense other
ideas, "a

form of taking
it all," after

all distraction
may be measured,

impossible
in quotes, are you

still writing you
ask, returning

from the river
with 4 bottles,

your fishing rod
and the pump, what

makes a vacuum
I think, as you

who disappear
into the dark,

a line of light
below the en-

trance she said, voice
like a pillow

my head touches,
one who calls from

Paris sounding
next door, in her

book "and he
spins around," five

on the next page
a title, follows

a light I see
looking up, O

moon, as something
may be said to

illuminate
all it touches,

rocks on the ground,
variations

on a theme by
someone, rhythm

for instance when
I step, who wants

to think about
how cells divide,

separation,
in a story

more than enough
reason not to,

or so it seems
to me now, sound

of water as
it fills the air,

ear that is, through
which it enters

one perception
of it, so that

all the rocks I
pick up, as weight

to be carried
on one's shoulders,

how the father
could be poisoned,

his brother now
wears his crown, who

asleep, as was
his custom in

the afternoon, say
will remember

what happened off
stage, beyond what

takes place in front
of us, we who

as audience
to Hamlet see,

hear about or
see and hear to-

gether simul-
taneously

so to speak, ghost's
speech and dumb show

remembering,
each in its own

way, what happened
before the play

actually
began, as if

Hamlet's father
were alive, sun

light moving down
slope facing east,

morning clouds gone,
each tree wanting

enough space, its
own area

in which to take
sustenance, spread

seed, as the cone
clusters on top

of those small firs
mean to do, I

think, feeling sun
on my back as

it climbs above
wall of canyon,

up which we will
be walking, each

syllable now
like a step, one

after the one
before it, where

logic might say
stop, keep going

in another
direction, how

rhythm itself,
disappearing

the moment one
stops thinking, will

equal desire
for it, even

if we don't know
that is so, what

I want, how I
am being when

the person you
are returns, home

being the place
I call it, this

place for instance
above the stream,

whose water makes
its own music,

constant, as if
Peter's blister

popped, the needle
having been burned

in a match, half
step between 3

and 4 and 1
and 7, twelve

bar blues in a
twelve tone scale, one

note's increment
each interval,

and the gods smiled
on someone who,

thrilling flowers,
delights in sun's

light, that lying
on a hot rock

after going
in, as body

half-submerged, sound
of it in one

ear, the other
person about

to mirror what
one is thinking,

you for instance
take two bottles,

pump, contemplate
where to go down

to fill them full
of water, that

is, having walked
to get to this

place by chance
this afternoon,

two o'clock, clouds
building in fine

print in blue pen
on this page, how

my hair begins
to dry in

this wind, color
of skin as it

absorbs the sun
imagine, how

it isn't its
sound exactly,

an ounce or two
at each pull, feet

exposed to air
beautiful, how

we walked in, not
on water fording

the south fork, if
this is it I

mean, not having
looked at the map

since yesterday
if then, I don't

remember mean-
ing to forget

lots of things, as
you reminded

me on a few
occasions, once

in a while so
to speak, as if

turning the page
could be next, one

word following
this one, one hour

ago having
arrived here, no

subtext except
time to go (to

be continued)
whenever I

think that is, this
in syllables

whose quadruple
time, as I call

it, makes a kind
of music or

how weathered wood
opens, breathes in

evolution,
the name of this

place, in a sense
the meaning is

most apparent
at this point, that

comma you just
heard as silence,

pause, however
lightly before

it continues
to the next line,

after which pause
again, again

continues to
continue, as

if to read this
text or hear it,

that being read
by someone else,

out loud, could be
equal to that

which it makes pre-
sent tense reading

it that is, as
I have written

this, a classic
mythology

perhaps, but one
I continue

to believe in,
waterfall now

we stop, someone
in a green shirt

beside the pool
it makes, filling

a couple of
bottles, before

we climb again
to the lake, say

the first person,
who is itself

part grammar, part
the way water

falling over
rocks goes silver,

white, mercury
as quickly as

it is written
here, a color

to find myself
in such a spot,

pumping water,
one on a rock

writing about
it, the other

spark connected,
meaning what is

happening be-
tween two bodies

separated
by distance, say

between spaces
one is walking

where I walk, write
it down I mean

to say, stopping
before I go

forward a few
more steps, like this

place and this pace,
letter missing

called l, which stands
for that person's

signature, how
the suddenly

lit west facing
mountain looks, its

draws and ridges
shadowed by sun-

light's last glimmer
as it fades, kind

of a desert
at this alti-

tude, sound of stream
at a distance

one has covered
on foot, each step

measured, not that
one imagines

a distance be-
yond it to be

so beautiful
it is moving,

breathing, thinking
at the same time

thoughts other than
this or that, which

as a person
prepares to photo-

graph the almost
full moon rising,

walking and breath-
ing together

as if terrain
or the person,

either one, could
somehow become

identical
so to speak, each

one merged, the star
above The Hermit

reflected, say
in mirror-like

lake's surface, say
before the cloud

covers it, rock
tapping on tent

peg, another
person thinking

what body, where
is the one it

means to counter,
such an oblique

reference, 3
syllables we

hear as 2, tired
in the shoulders

feeling a stretch
will relax, help

to finish an-
other day as

they say, that I
can be the sound

of thought itself
I think, thinking

the sound of what
is passing in-

terior, plane
one hears whose sound

follows its light,
velocity

measured in miles
per second, I

am guessing, per
second meaning

how quiet it
is, no birds or

even falling
water, only

moonlight on its
fluent route, as

if one- or two-
dimensional

space, visible
as it rides in

to the night, I
thinking of you

until it sees
you beside me,

temperature
rising, sun's light

on granite like
a table, sloped

to face it as
ants, a chipmunk

of some sort, make
an appearance

being at home
here, an effect

dreams register
as I wake, that

it doesn't make
sense to be do-

ing this, a curve
of line where you

cast it, its sound
a kind of spin

of line in air's
elastic, each

next thought, the way
I think of you

as opposed to
how you are, say

at the door or
once, in a chair

unable to
think, how you looked

directly to-
ward the person

I am, someone
in the mirror

of relation-
ship with someone

who is not that
person, equal

that is to what
thinking is, where

surface ripples
mean wind, a shift

in person for
instance, present

tense, how it is
likely that I

will continue
to be so, one

equal to one,
the other as

much a part, say
of this figure

of speech, as it
can in cases

become, looking
at the map for

example, how
elevation

can be written
as lines, contour

at intervals
of 50 feet,

only 3 feet
to the ground, which

one hits having
stumbled, ahead

of oneself, so
maybe the foot

didn't lift it-
self suddenly

falling, what was
I thinking of

but you, how could
that have happened

written at 12
thousand feet, Muir

Pass named for you
know who, that is

some of you will
know, that a man

can orient
a map, what he

thinks is east is
indeed east, both

persons meaning
to adjust, lift

or shorten straps
or slides, shoulders

feeling the weight
disappear, ear

cut where one fell
on it, as if

still asleep, or
did such a thing

even happen
as I say, past

tense suspect per-
haps given that

everything is
still going for-

ward the song says,
say that lakes are

visible at
some point, elsewhere

against the rocks
ultra vio-

let sunlight, form
of the poem

preceding its
next thought, so the

person writing
imagines, rock

sounding as foot
comes down, about

to be leaving
this place, the left

hand page, meaning
the audience

whereupon he
almost falls, as

I in fact did,
so distracted

by everything
I'm thinking, left

hand curve of trail
in the hot sun-

light, beginning
to understand

the form of the
poem, thinking

in syllables
like this, liquid

flowing under
rocks, tongue and lips

dry, how it is
that altitude

does this, as if
oxygen wants

another name
for itself, sun

on the backs of
my legs, knees that

is, stopping at
the lake's outflow

to talk a bit
to someone, clean

place to pump, stain
of sweat white on

Pete's green shirt, his
other bottle

in a pocket
on the rock, which

in spite of it-
self hesitates

to speak, echoes
ears are burning

so, as thinking
to say mistakes

I have made, how
wanting you back

means it, feeling
literally

light headed when
I get to green-

matter, water
instinct even

if one isn't
a water sign,

strenuous go-
ing overland

on southern ap-
proach to Muir Pass

I mean, where a
marmot if there

ever was one
can disappear, it's

all been a mis-
take I repeat

on the right hand
page, that itself

has spoken, the
spell or should I

say smell of short-
needled Jeffrey

pine, if it is
technically

speaking that, the
rock with the spot

about balance,
one body in

relation to
another, as

sunlight become
shade, a shadow

foliage casts
passing under-

neath it, sylvan
historian

as Wordsworth meant
to say, nameless

lake at the base
of beautiful

steep descent through
trees, wildflowers

again even
though it's past mid-

August, yellow
and violet

and blue petals
in clumps, and there's

an Indian
paintbrush, the Black

Divide above
Camp 4 for in-

stance at this time
of day, a half

hour or so be-
fore the sun goes

down, already
back of the ridge

west of here, hear
no difference

between the stream
close to it, far

away, almost
the full moon placed

midway between
two ridges, one

still sunlit, the
other shadowed

facing away
from it, how it

suddenly ap-
pears without one

noticing it
has risen, "how

silently and
with how wan," as

Sidney writes, a
face that itself

appears to be
one, the final

light as it leaves
the ridge, which I

don't know beyond
which in a few

days cars, traffic
on the road home

wherever it
is, for instance

the person in
it in the mid-

dle of a night
I wake to, who

else besides you
might I be think-

ing of, I mean
you understand

me, myself not
simply the one

who transcribes what
I'm given, why

this thought instead
of that, birdwing

or was it bat
flits by, present

now if only
in theory, which

can be pleasure
as well, that a

mere satellite
appears to dis-

place space, as if
laterally

moving against
the sky, other

stars' gradual
rotation, cold

as night falls on
what I write, how

what is equal
to that goes, say

the sun comes up
by degrees north-

east of where moon
rose last night, I

mean to connect
this thought, though it's

secondary
perhaps to be-

ing in the same
place I am, how

suddenly one
becomes ten, quote

unquote, the mother
who walks her child

to the big o-
cean I thought once

to call it, that
memory can

if it will re-
member of what

one wants, someone
with whom it all

seemingly con-
nects in the sense

that one makes one-
self the other's

image, as I
sees itself say

in the pronoun
you, for instance

you are drinking
coffee, reading

the paper, the
other who thinks

this is so makes
it so, if that

isn't too much
to suppose, how

the sound of what
one first hears is-

n't the stream of
a jet, about

to be moving
down canyon, sound

again all that
registers per-

haps can say, to
be continued

50 minutes
from there, log

upon which one
contemplates what-

ever comes to
mind, avalanche

signs including
fallen stumps, each

adjustment an
object of end-

less interest so
called, O reader

hyphen listen-
er whoever

you are, a line
between granite

spire and crystal
blues of sky fill-

ing this line, say
one is walking

ahead, the one
who follows keep-

ing score as it
were, the record

revolving at
its sound's speed, say

I am thinking
this, such a place

at such a time
of the day who-

ever I am
again, rhythm's

repetition
as we know, which

peak is that one
on the map, Pete

asks, taking it
out to look at

topographic
politics, twin

knifelines define
Langille Peak, so

called, named after
somebody it

would appear, one
having claimed it

I imagine
in language, whose

circumference
can define it-

self in terms of
distance, seeing

its curve from an-
other angle

here, Langille by
another name

as skin, hands grasp
quadriceps and

hamstring, pulling
one up to this

gnarled juniper's
shade, at which point

one takes a look
at Langille a-

cross an expanse
of sheer space, in

whose emptiness
one becomes breath-

less, exertion
like this the way

the body knows
itself, person

too, the I you
contemplate as

being living
as Stein wrote, not

that it matters
here being mere-

ly what I am do-
ing so to speak

here, now present
indicative

the tense for ex-
ample being

words that just came
to mind, Langille

Peak another
perspective, one

point, how many
eyes does it take

to see this, how
many bottles

will you pump, one
taking a break

facing south, one
forty-five this

afternoon, back
to work pumping

as one leans back
into sunlight,

water music
in A sharp, flat

rock, another
one on which

if I wash my-
self I will dry

in the sun I
will see, I mean

the real spring, well
in which the fish

lives, under rocks
in the middle

of the day, so
beautifully

marked when you re-
move the metal

from its mouth, red
orange spots on

its side, which is
streaked with rainbow

green and golden
brown, as lesson

in trout in season
say, as the wind

lifts my shirt, dry
after 20

minutes on that
rock, waterfall

that washed me, pen
drying out in

hot sun, double
intensity

at this alti-
tude as someone

said, a flower
the essence of

yellow, liquid
amber trunks on

weathered pine I
recall, too long

ago, from 9
to 12 thousand

feet today, bear
cub in LeConte

Canyon, "rolled round in
earth's diurnal

course with rocks and
stones and trees" Words-

worth wrote, mountains
in motion it

would seem, glacier
having scoured that

basin south of
Langille Peak, up

which one could scram-
ble from the looks

of it at this
distance, sunlit

faces, others
already in

shade as the sun
moves west, left knee

beginning to feel
it, the habits

of fish, as two
in such a small

stream can live
happily, at

3:15 it's
almost time, high

elevation
light, this drainage

green, meaning that
one is pointing

to a place to
stop, idea's

mirror the way
stream bends, grasses

as green as eye
can see, I miss

having a knife
you say, reaching

for the next best
thing, which is a

fork, with which one
can untangle

the line, its measure
coming to mind

without thinking
even, simply

let each moment
drive, listener

beside the sound
of water, or

water itself
say in paren-

thesis, this scene
for example

what I am think-
ing on paper

in blue pen, as
you are reading

it later, when
I am gone as

the poets used
to say, Ronsard's

"when you are old
and grey and sit-

ting by the fire,"
as Yeats translates

it, trout jumping
when grasses bend

followed by an
ellipsis, Pan

would have been hap-
py in this place

you say, meaning
it's idyllic

as can be, so
possible say

to say it this
wrongly, as on

my shin an inch
worm maybe, one

head in the bush-
es coming back

from fish, the one
even I see

darting away
into shade, wind

hardly a fact-
or in any

case, syllables
equal to each

other, the line
like a flashing

of whip in the
sun, I'm ready

when you are you
say, seeing it's

about time, how
the trail follows

the stripe in the
rock, this garden

consisting of
pyramid, square

and rectangle
beyond which, strange

like liquid shapes
of tree, or what's

left of it nest-
led into rock's

crook, walking long
enough to find

myself in this
place, Bishop Pass

within range to-
morrow morning

as I say, which
is where I want

to stop writing
I think, signal

by whistling I'm
here, a campsite

with a granite
table, stone chairs

from which to watch
the sun's depart-

ure behind that
35 de-

gree slope, moon full
or a minute

after, between
Isoceles

Peak and I don't
know what, the sound

of zippers and
a fish jumps, just

as I thought it
would, leaning back

with a cup of
tea and honey

a lemon drop
dissolves in, as

you who love to
be, period

before the quote
astonished, as

if it's getting
light again, moon's

light that is re-
flected off that

peak opposite
this view, one point

perspective so
called, bird meaning

cries in empty
space, contemplate

stars in the Dip-
per's handle start

to turn, return
tomorrow to

what I left, so
quiet tonight

ear's asleep, eye
sees the planet

descending, or
so at least it

seems, avalanche
path where nothing

will grow, and let
me not forget

the person whose
picture I car-

ry in mind so
to speak, as far

from here as pos-
sible given

the size of this
planet, as if

I possibly
could, growing cold

except that rocks
facing the set-

ting sun stay warm
a long time, there

goes Jupiter,
Venus or who

knows what star, Black
Divide so called

for obvious
reasons, one sees

that is a tone
of voice, the ear

watches what is
happening, that

how she enters
a room aimless-

ly, begins to
speak but decides

not to, candle
on granite ledge

beside my right
shoulder, further

than ever sound
plummeted, lets

be as Hamlet
the son real-

izes, too late
perhaps but so

what, the actor
or should I say

character has
a point, patience

you say except
it's late for ex-

amples in this
case, "with how sad

steps O moon thou
climb'st the skies, how

silently, and
with how wan a

face" as Sidney
wrote, I repeat

in Astrophel
and Stella, I

mean, getting up
at dawn the moon

above the Black
Divide, whose ridge

is itself get-
ting first sunlight

from the east, shape
of peaks casting

their shadows as
disk of moon dis-

appears behind
it, so that it

looms, having been
arranged as it

were by nature
itself, if one

might be allowed
that, natural

forces in an-
y case being

something to con-
template from time

to time, "shadows
on a moving

picture screen," as
Robert Duncan

described our life
after Sir Walt-

er Ralegh, in
whose footsteps he

was pleased to walk
of course, dream of

the wife who shows
me her hips, black

with blue from weight
of pack, last night's

camp 11,
000 feet plus

that is, smaller
branches on high

altitute pine
stopped, as if all

that happens here
conditions what-

ever shape they
assume, reading

patches of green
on the slope, as

if light was on
it, ice crystal

on the inside
of tent fly mean-

ing it was cold-
er last night than

one thought, fingers
on ridge of peak

Columbine could
be over twen-

ty feet, at this
distance who can

tell, primitive
ritual of

washing one's hands
at the well, last

details like plas-
tic on the ground

or a loose shoe-
lace before you

begin, a friend
who carries his

friend's collection
of rocks, above

the treeline be-
yond any call

of duty I
mean, weight balanced

after all, one
breath per step up

this steep, inhaled
the oxygen

body wanted
suddenly ex-

haled too, the grade
approaching the

pass lifting it-
self along lines

map registers
closer, contours

meaning pitch, how
the line stops by

turning the cor-
ner to reverse

direction, left
margin merely

a place to start
another for-

ward motion, fish
story of how

trout took the fly
in a pool, pass

moving figures
human, someone

where I will stop
this, contemplate

view of Mount A-
gassiz's massive

faces, divide's
planetary

wind meaning it
is spinning, in

which direction
I don't know, west

to east, not that
any words make

a difference
to wind, those two

on a grid whose
dimensions in-

clude horizon-
tal extending

the vertical
clear to blue, how

recently snow
covered the switch-

backs, underground
sound of water

boulders channel
below you, who

notices it
stopping, poem's

sense of itself
being exact-

ly in place, where
words in the world

intersect I
mean to say, thought

over which I
have little con-

trol, play as it
were a minor

part, simply feet
walking a line

down the page, a
place where water

crosses it, say
it will be time

to stop, sit back
a bit to see

the light surround-
ing all of us

say, "for Christ's sake
look out where you're

going" as Cree-
ley reminds me

here, ears open
to what's about

to take place or
is now happen-

ing, as nothing
is but thinking

makes it so, thanks
to Hamlet for

that, who loves to
be astonished

again and a-
gain meaning that

repetition
informs the form-

ula it it-
self meditates

upon, that 4
syllables in

continuous
lines, these 4 for

instance make lit-
tle difference

in the world,
how the body

will want swallows
of water be-

fore I stop, this
lake isn't South

Lake, which is still
somewhere ahead

of where I think
it will be, that

object for ex-
ample that casts

its shadow, tree
or rock subject

to nothing writ-
ing alone makes

of it, as thought
itself is one

way of taking
it all in, as

if one means to
do that, one or

two syllables
maybe, 3 or

4 more perhaps
until it's fin-

ished, which is what
I mean to do

more or less less
than before, that

in quotations,
a car waiting

to carry me
home, how open

vowels sound the
wind, making its

way, the person
I am present

to, following
in steps others

have taken, sound
of a plane now

close at hand, so
subjectively

thinking of what
to say, a lake's

water bluer
than sky, my friend

stopping to look
down at it, I

who also stop
thinking this, that

is, what might be
in syllables

meant by this, this
being the end

More Rocks was written on a backpacking trip in the Sierra Nevada between North Lake and South Lake, 60 miles over three 12,000-foot passes August 15–21, 1994. I wrote in two-line stanzas (four syllables in each line, a mark of punctuation in each pair of lines) as a kind of walking meditation.